THE FLINTSTONES

by JERRY BECK

INSIGHT EDITIONS

San Rafael, CA

CONTENTS

The inspiration for *The Flintstones* came in 1959, when producers at Columbia Pictures decided to develop a prime-time animated sitcom. At the time Columbia was offering TV networks a stream of popular prime-time sitcoms (*Father Knows Best, Donna Reed, Dennis the Menace*) and animated children's shows such as *Huckleberry Hound* and *Yogi Bear*. To combine the two concepts, Columbia naturally looked to Bill Hanna and Joe Barbera—the dynamic duo behind Huckleberry Hound, Yogi Bear, and a host of other animated hits. After taking on the job, Hanna-Barbera decided to center the show on a family and tried out families composed of farmers, hillbillies, and even ancient Romans. Nothing really worked until H-B artist Dan Gordon sketched a couple of cavemen in animal skins. Character designer Ed Benedict refined the characters into the first crude version of the Flintstone family—originally named the Flagstones—and history was made. It was decided to place the characters in a mythical town called Bedrock, and by early 1960 Hanna and Barbera had enough of a concept in place to pitch the show to potential buyers.

The Flagstones was purchased by ABC. By then, the name of the show had been changed to *The Flintstones* to avoid confusion with another family appearing in a popular comic strip (the Flagstones were

SIS   GRANNY   JETHRO   ZACK

2

FOUNDLING HOME

10

FL-1

N-1

WILMA

featured in Hi & Lois). The first episode of the series, "*The Flintstone Flyer*," aired on September 30, 1960. That evening America became acquainted with Fred Flintstone, his wife Wilma, and best friends Barney and Betty Rubble. These Stone Age citizens lived in a world of appliances powered by animals, houses and offices constructed out of boulders, and cars that ran on foot power. Against this backdrop the likeable characters lived out typical suburban lives with a sitcom twist.

Audiences immediately loved the show, and a nation took the Flintstones to heart. Millions laughed at Fred's exuberant "Yabba Dabba Doo!" and tuned in to see what not-so-clever schemes Fred and Barney were attempting to put over on their wives. As the show evolved over time, it became even more popular. When Wilma gave birth to Pebbles Flintstone on February 22, 10,000 BC (1963 to us), a record number of viewers tuned in. Within weeks, stores sold out

Flintstones, meet the Flintstones,
They're the modern Stone Age family
From the town of Bedrock,
They're a page right out of history

Let's ride with the family down the street,
Through the courtesy of Fred's two feet

When you're with the Flintstones,
Have a Yabba-Dabba-Doo time,
A Dabba-Doo time,
You'll have a gay old time!

Theme Song - Lyrics by William Hanna and Joe Barbera
Music by Hoyt Curtin

of Pebbles dolls. Hanna and Barbera's writing staff featured cartoon veterans such as Warren Foster and Michael Maltese. Stories could include celebrities, science-fiction and fantasy themes, or parodies of popular culture to the delight of TV audiences. Anything could happen in Bedrock!

Soon it seemed that everyone could quote a favorite episode. Flintstones toys, collectibles, and licensed products were found in virtually every home. Most memorable of all was the show's theme song, *Meet the Flintstones,* originally written by Hoyt Curtin for a novelty record based on the show. It became so popular that it replaced the original opening theme song, *"Rise and Shine"* in 1962. Anyone who doesn't know the tune and lyrics by now must be, well, living in a cave.

The Flintstones would go on to star in a full-length theatrical feature, *A Man Called Flintstone,* in 1966. Although the TV show was cancelled in that same year, it proved impossible to keep a good caveman down. 1971 saw the Saturday morning debut of *The Pebbles and Bamm-Bamm Show,* which featured teenage versions of the famous kids. The next year brought *The Flintstones Comedy Hour.* The prehistoric family starred in their first Christmas special in 1978 and to this day the Flintstones are rarely absent from TV.

In 1987, the Flintstones met their Space Age counterparts, the Jetsons, in a two-hour television movie. With the advent of the *Cartoon Network* in 1992, modern writers and artists continued to riff on the "modern Stone Age family" and in 1994, a live action movie was a huge hit in theaters around the world. *The Flintstones* was the longest running animated prime-time television show in U.S. history until *The Simpsons* set a new record for episodes thirty-one years later. Over the course of their six seasons and 166 episodes, *The Flintstones* went from unexpected hit to a set of beloved icons. *The Flintstones* truly remain the first family of American animation. Yabba-Dabba-Doo!

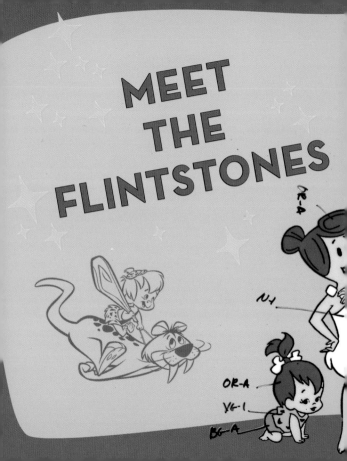

We can only guess at what life was like in the Stone Age, but if the Flintstones were a typical family of the time their lives were not much different than ours!

When we meet family patriarch Fred Flintstone, we learn that he lives in the suburb of Bedrock and works at the local quarry as a dino-crane operator. Big of heart (and stomach), Fred is a loving husband, loyal friend and proud father. Waiting for him in their boulder-shaped home is his red-haired wife, Wilma. Her patience with Fred's moods, schemes, and rough edges is boundless. Their daughter, Pebbles, a sweetly cooing baby girl, absolutely loves her Daddy, so does family pet Dino, a peppy, purple Snorkasaurus, who bowls Fred over every time his master comes home.

Right next door to Fred we find Barney and Betty Rubble, the Flintstone's best friends. Barney tries to be the voice of reason when Fred hatches his plots, but that doesn't stop poor Barney from getting into his share of trouble as well. Betty's infectious giggle can be heard all the way down to the local mall where she and Wilma shop together—when not keeping an eye on their mischievous hubbies. Betty and Barney have adopted a boy named Bamm-Bamm—also known as the world's strongest baby. Like many neighbors, the Flintstones and the Rubbles have their share of disputes and misunderstandings, but in the end, nothing could really shake their deep friendships.

Bedrock is also home to many supporting characters such as Fred's boss, Mr. Slate; Wilma's mother, Mrs. Slaghoople; Arnold the paperboy, a weird family of neighbors called the Gruesomes, and Fred's lodge brothers in The Loyal Order of the Water Buffalos. In addition, Fred and Barney met up with both fictitious and real-life celebrities in cartoon form. Actress Ann Margret (as Ann Margrock), bandleader Hoagy Carmichael, Tony Curtis (as Stoney Curtis) and Samantha (Elizabeth Montgomery) from Bewitched made memorable one-shot appearances in the stone-age community. An alien-in-exile known as The Great Gazoo also visited Bedrock on a regular basis in the last season, granting Fred and Barney magic wishes which often had disastrous results. Gazoo's magical antics—such as making Fred the boss of the Gravel Pit, turning him into a ballerina or changing Barney into a woman—helped transform the animated sitcom from a traditional adult-skewed domestic comedy to a kid-friendly fantasy.

20 Celebrities and characters spoofed on *The Flintstones*:

Stoney Curtis	(Tony Curtis)
Ann-Margrock	(Ann-Margaret)
Peter Gunnite	(Peter Gunn)
Cary Granite	(Cary Grant)
Arthur Quarry	(Arthur Murray)
Alvin Brickrock	(Alfred Hitchcoock)
Sassie	(Lassie)
Dripper	(Flipper)
Dr. Ben Casement	(Dr. Ben Casey)
Conrad Hailstone	(Conrad Hilton)
Lollobrickada	(Gina Lollobrigida)
Perry Masonry	(Perry Mason)
Dr. Sigrock Freep	(Dr.Sigmund Freud)
Ed Sullystone	(Ed Sullivan)
Adobe Dick	(Moby Dick)
The Cartrocks	(The Cartwrights of Bonanza)
Eppy Brianstone	(Brain Epstein)
Jimmy Darrock	(James Darren)
Samantha and Darrin from Bewitched	(Elizabeth Montgomery and Dick York)

THE FLINTSTONES THROUGH THE AGES

1940 Story artist Dan Gordon begins writing a series of "Stone Age Cartoons" for Fleischer Studios, which contain spot-gags of cavemen spoofing the conventions of modern life.

1955 Designer Ed Benedict designs an MGM Tex Avery cartoon, "The First Bad Man"—a western spoof enacted by cavemen.

1959 Story artist Dan Gordon sketches some new Stone Age gags for Hanna-Barbera as a proposal for a new TV series. Barbera hands them to designer Ed Benedict who defines the lead characters. Gordon, Barbera and Michael Maltese write the pilot episode, then known as *The Flagstones*.

1960 Hanna and Barbera pitch the show to ABC. The show is sold as a prime-time series to debut in September.

1960 Alan Reed (Fred), Mel Blanc (Barney), Jean Vander Pyl (Wilma), and Bea Benederet (Betty) begin voicing the cast of *The Flintstones*. The first episode a on September 30th, 1960.

1961 The episode "The Snorkasaurus Hunter" tells the story of how Dino joined the family.

1962 The theme song "Meet the Flintstones" begins with the third season episodes.

1963 Pebbles is born and Bamm-Bamm is adopted. Gerry Johnson replaces Bea Benederet as Betty.

1964 *The Gruesomes*, the Flintstones' new neighbors, are introduced.

1965 The Great Gazoo first appears.

1966 The ABC prime-time series is cancelled. Columbia Pictures releases *The Man Called Flintstone*—the first Flintstones feature length movie.

THE MAN CALLED FLINTSTONE

1967 NBC puts *The Flintstones* (reruns) on Saturday morning, and Screen Gems syndicates the series to local TV stations.

1968 *Flintstones Chewable Vitamins* are introduced by Bayer.

1971 *The Pebbles and Bamm-Bamm Show* (CBS) debuts featuring teenage Pebbles (voiced by Sally Struthers) and Bamm-Bamm (voiced by Jay North). Pebbles Cereal is introduced by Post.

1972 *The Flintstone Comedy Hour* runs on CBS, as do reruns of both *The Flintstones* and *The Pebbles & Bamm Bamm Show*.

1977 *Fred Flintstone and Friends* airs in first-run syndication. Henry Corden takes over as the voice of Fred Flintstone. The TV special, *A Flintstone Christmas*, airs on NBC. Fred and Barney make appearances on *Scooby's All-Star Laff-a-Lympics* (ABC series).

1978 The Flintstones: Little Big League TV special airs on NBC.

1979 The New Fred and Barney Show, Fred and Barney Meet the Thing, and Fred and Barney Meet the Shmoo all air on NBC.

1980 The Flintstone Comedy Show airs on NBC with segments "The Bedrock Cops," "Pebbles, Dino and Bamm-Bamm," "Captain Caveman," "The Flintstones Family Album," "Dino and Cavemouse" and "The Frankenstones." Two NBC TV specials—The Flintstones' New Neighbors and The Flintstones Meet Rockula and Frankenstone—premiere.

1981 Three more NBC TV specials are made—The Flintstones: Fred's Final Fling, The Flintstones: Wind-Up Wilma and The Flintstones: Jogging Fever.

1982 The Flintstone Funnies (NBC) repackages various Flintstones episodes into a new format for Saturday morning viewers.

1986 The Flintstone Kids (ABC)—a new Saturday morning series featuring the Flintstones and Rubbles as kids premieres. An NBC special called The Flintstoes 25th Anniversary Celebration is hosted by Tim Conway, Harvey Korman and Vanna White.

1987 In the made for TV movie, *The Jetsons Meet the Flintstones*, the two animated prime-time families meet up in an historic, time-warping mash-up.

1988 *The Flintstones Kids' "Just Say No" Special* runs on ABC. The highly acclaimed and award-winning special used the prehistoric preteens and former first lady Nancy Reagan to address a very modern issue of drug abuse.

1993 Pebbles and Bamm-Bamm marry in *I Yabba Dabba Do!* (an ABC made for TV movie). Pebbles and Bamm-Bamm have a baby in *Hollyrock-A-Bye Baby* (another ABC made for TV movie). The TV special, *The Flintstone Family Christmas*, airs on ABC.

1994 The live action Universal movie, *The Flintstones*, grosses a record-breaking $37.5 million in its opening weekend. *A Flintstones' Christmas Carol* premieres on TV.

1995 Dino appears in two Cartoon Network world premiere cartoons directed by Joe Barbera: "Stay Out" and "The Great Egg-Scape."

1996 *Cave Kids: Pebbles & Bamm Bamm* runs on PBS.

2000 Universal releases a sequel to *The Flintstones* titled *The Flintstones in Viva Rock Vegas*.

2001 A new Flintstones made for TV movie, *The Flintstones: On The Rocks* premieres on the Cartoon Network.

Lovable tots Pebbles Flintstone and Bamm-Bamm Rubble grew up to star in *The Pebbles and Bamm-Bamm Show* and later got married and had a baby in their very own TV special. Even here there was something between them!

When Bamm-Bamm finally proposed it was time for a family celebration—and the wedding of the year. With everyone in their finest ... and a rock band playing (naturally).

There were special guests ... and even an anachronistic honeymoon!

17 Paul Drive : San Rafael : CA : 94903
www.insighteditions.com
phone 415.526.1370 : fax 415.526.1394

Library of Congress Cataloging-in-Publication Data available.
ISBN-13: 978-1-933784-60-1

Insight Editions would like to extend a special thanks to Ruth Clampett and
Clampett Studio Collections (www.clampettstudio.com) and Mike Van Eaton
and Van Eaton Galleries (www.vegalleries.com) for their help in putting
together the Insight Mini-Classics series.

ROOTS of PEACE   REPLANTED PAPER

Palace Press International, in association with Roots of Peace, will plant two trees for each
tree used in the manufacturing of this book. Roots of Peace is an internationally renowned
humanitarian organization dedicated to eradicating land mines worldwide and converting
war-torn lands into productive farms and wildlife habitats. Together, we will plant two
million fruit and nut trees in Afghanistan and provide farmers there with the skills and
support necessary for sustainable land use.

10 9 8 7 6 5 4 3 2 1

Printed in China by Palace Press International